CELEBRATE
ᵗHE DAYS

BROTHER THOMAS
BOOK ᴼF DAYS

CREDITS:

Design: Leslie Anne Feagley

Editor: Jeanne Gressler

Photography: Max Coniglio

COVER:

TEA BOWL, square form, Tenmoku with Crystal Rutile Glaze, $3\frac{3}{4}$ x $4\frac{5}{8}$ x $4\frac{5}{8}$", TH1548

FRONTISPIECE:

TEA BOWL, Molybdenum Glaze, $3\frac{1}{4}$ x $4\frac{3}{4}$ x $4\frac{3}{4}$" TH1558

ISBN 1-879985-05-5

PUCKER GALLERY

171 Newbury Street

Boston, MA 02116

(617) 267-9473

fax: (617) 424-9759

email: contactus@puckergallery.com

www.puckergallery.com

CELEBRATE
the DAYS

BROTHER THOMAS
BOOK of DAYS

REFLECTIONS
ON THE CUP

נַעֲשֶׂה וְנִשְׁמָע

On the one hand, there is this obvious thing about a cup, i.e., it is an object to hold a liquid, a vessel from which we drink. This is the cup as a useful good, what the ancients called a *bonum utile.* The good of it is its functional value to us.

But on the other hand, there is another thing about a cup of which we are less immediately conscious — its transcendent good, its *bonum honestum.* It can sign something over and above its useful good. Whether it is a primitive drinking gourd, a teacup, a coffee cup or a formal ritual vessel, in the order of symbol, they are all vessels of hospitality and celebration. And that purpose transcends their obvious function.

We gather around the cup to share ourselves, to tell our stories, to sing our songs. With scarcely a conscious thought we welcome a friend, a guest with a cup of tea, a cup of coffee, a glass of wine. This spontaneous cup-of-welcome is a primal ritual which celebrates a relationship, something over and above its function. Moreover, it is a custom so old and so cross-cultural that it touches what is common in us despite what is different between us.

And, among those things-in-common is an innate human need to make those "cups of welcome" as beautiful as they are functional. The beautiful itself serves a higher function. The beautiful is at the center of every civilization in its art, its music, its architecture, its people.

There is no reason that what is functional, the *bonum utile*, the useful good, cannot co-exist with the *bonum honestum*, what is good in itself. Otherwise a galvanized bucket would be just as good to hold flowers as a beautiful Song dynasty vase. The Song vase brings the same function, the *bonum utile* as the bucket does, but also something the bucket does not, *i.e.*, aesthetic beauty, the *bonum honestum*.

Even the most primitive vessels of primordial peoples have their decorative scratches added to them. They add nothing to the function; they add to the human spirit. The human seed has an appetite for the beautiful.

That is why in the best of ceramic art neither function nor beauty can be repealed; it is the commission of this art to bond the two of them. It is not a thing of reason; it is a thing of the heart. This bond of function and beauty is an essential part of the cups of celebration of every culture, and in particular with those cups of East and West cultures with which we are most familiar: the Christian chalice, the Jewish kiddish cup, the Japanese chawan.

My personal life has been involved with all three of these formal vessels, so they show up now and then, here and there, in my work as a potter. I take deep pleasure and feel privileged to be able to make them, because apart from their differences and those rationalities which dictate what they should be and what they should not be, they all call forth this one thing that transcends all other things: they ought to be beautiful. And that touches my commission as an artist. As an artist that is the work of my soul, my work in the world. The history, the theology, the canons of ritual vessels are best left to others.

For the sake of consistency with the images used in this Day Book, I need to limit my personal reflections to one ritual vessel, the tea bowl. My experience with making the chalice and the Kiddish cup will have to be bracketed for now, reserved for a later opportunity.

It is said, and from a potter's bias, I believe it is true to say, that the tea bowl or chawan is the most revered item of the Japanese tea ceremony; perhaps even more central than the tea itself. While both the tea and tea bowl were brought to Japan from China, probably by Japanese monks, the tea ceremony was not. It is a uniquely Japanese ritual. In China the "ceremony" which the Japanese monks encountered was apparently a tea contest:

THE DARK COLOR OF THE GLAZE MADE THEM ESPECIALLY SUITABLE FOR THE TEA TESTING COMPETITIONS WHICH WERE IN FASHION IN THE SONG PERIOD, THE OBJECT OF THE CONTEST TO SEE WHOSE TEA WOULD STAND THE LARGEST NUMBER OF WATERINGS AND IT WAS FOUND THAT THE LEAST TRACE OF TEA WAS FOUND VISIBLE AGAINST THE BLACK GLAZE OF THE CHIEN BOWLS.

...THE CHINESE TEA CONTESTS WERE ADOPTED BY THE JAPANESE, WHO ELABORATED THEM INTO THE CURIOUS CEREMONY KNOWN AS CHA NO YU.[1]

———————————

In China these rich black Chien yao bowls were primarily pragmatic elements of the tea contest, although doubtlessly they were also prized for their beauty since so many of them have been preserved over the centuries despite destruction in China and Chinese destructiveness itself.

By contrast, the "curious ceremony" of the Japanese evolved more and more into a ritual witness to Zen Buddhist principles of awakening to, and awareness of

[1] Hobson, R.L. Chinese Pottery and Porcelain, Vol. 1, Dover, NY, 1975, p. 131.

the humanizing values of harmony, respect, purity and tranquility. Needless to say, but it helps to say it, these values are not exclusively Japanese or Zen. They are universally humanizing values, which is to say, they are spiritual values.

A beautiful tea bowl in this context transcends its practical function; it interfaces art and religion which is what great art has always done, and does still even if, regrettably, that is not so evident in today's dwindling culture:

RELIGION AND ART WENT HAND IN HAND FOR SO MANY CENTURIES. ALAS, TODAY RELIGION HAS LOST ITS SENSE OF ART AND ART HAS LOST ITS SENSE OF RELIGION.[2]

In the climate of globalization in which we now live, it is not surprising that the meaning of tea and the tea ceremony itself should migrate west. The principles of Zen peace echo western religious principles of interiority: prayer, silence, and solitude. Both oppose our present cul-ture of mindless noise that drowns out the inner voice.

In C.S. Lewis's little big book, <u>The Screwtape Letters</u>, the principal characters are Screwtape and Wormwood. Screwtape is a kind of supervisor devil trying to instruct by mail his novice devil named Wormwood. Wormwood is totally inept and fails to carry out all the instructions for debasing his victims. Finally, in desperation, Screwtape tells the novice Wormwood, "...give them noise." And, we got it – in music, in art, in film, in literature, in the home, in the streets. Nothing makes room for noise like a lack of interiority and nothing destroys interiority as completely as noise. Serene rituals such as the tea ceremony, "curious" or not, call us to reflect on the spiritual values without which our species will not survive.

It is important that the tea bowl be a vessel of function but also it must be a thing of spirit, which is to say, beautiful. Without the spirit of the beautiful the voice of the ritual would at least be dimin-

[2] Bezanson, Brother Thomas, "Art and Religious Experience", <u>Creation out of Clay</u>, Pucker Gallery, Boston, MA and Wm. B. Eerdmans, Grand Rapids, MI, 1999, p. 56.

ished if not completely silenced. The ugly is a kind of aesthetic noise.

But then, there is the unarguable reality of "taste," i.e., what is beautiful to one person may not be beautiful to another. In the end, what does that matter? It may be itself spiritual growth to broaden our vision by openness to another's vision. We do not all see through the same lens. If we cannot see beauty in the thing itself, perhaps we can see the beauty in the person seeing beauty in the thing. That in the end is what will transform the world. The world at its quantum foundations is not predictability but possibility. The beautiful is an attribute of that ultimate reality, by whatever name we call it, and it is infinitely diverse. Openness is fundamental to seeing it.

I had not been familiar with tea bowls, much less the tea ceremony, before my first visit to Japan in 1978. America does not have a tea culture and in my native land of Nova Scotia, where tea drinking was more common, the only ritual was whether the milk went into the cup before or after the tea. And, we custom-

arily drank tea out of those bone china teacups by Wedgewood and Spode or their imitations for kitchen-level use. It is an odd evolution since English teacups were originally imitations of Chinese tea bowls that had acquired a little handle and English bone china was an attempt to imitate oriental porcelain. Evolution is not always a straight line; there are a few circles in there.

But, during that early exposure to Japan, the tea bowl, teacup, (yu no mi) and tea drinking were omnipresent. A cup of tea was a standard welcome. In fact, there was often no charge in a restaurant for Ocha, ordinary green tea. I was especially struck by the ritual tea bowls, the Chawan. They were beautiful and important to Japanese art and lifestyle. I was moved also that individual artists and regions were recognized and celebrated for their tea bowls.

As a potter, those twenty and some years ago I was drawn to the tea bowls but I was also present to the Zen dimension of their use in the tea ceremony, *i.e.*, that bond between the *bonum utile* and the *bonum honestum,* between art and religion. It was an old experience rediscovered in a new way. I tucked it away in my spirit because it was a spiritual experience.

As the temperature of cultural and religious meeting had been rising during those years it was not entirely surprising to find westerners on a spiritual quest studying Zen in Japan. Nor was it surprising that young westerners were there studying pottery with Japanese masters, *sensei.* And, in the way of things it is not surprising that these separate quests should return home to give root and reason in this country for tea bowls, tea ceremony, and Zen values. It hasn't revolutionized art or religion in America but it has enriched them — or can. Openness again, that nexus of the spirit is needed for that.

When in the course of my own events, I was asked to make tea bowls, the spiritual resonance I had with tea bowls so many years before was still there. I knew I had to grow into them, not technically, but interiorily — *na'a sheh v'nishma* (let us do it and we will understand).

These bowls are like a chalice, a kiddish cup — they are symbols of something beyond them. They are not run out by the dozens, not made exactly, but born of a person's spirit. They have to be about something beyond but added to function. That is why a tea bowl is called by a name in Japan, often poetic names, more often by the name of the artist who made it, e.g., an Arakawa, a Shimaoka, a Hamada, a Fugiwara.... When that meeting of spirits happens, perhaps some tea master calls a special bowl to celebrate the tea ceremony or some ordinary person simply loves it, makes tea and quietly celebrates a moment. For every moment of life is worthy of celebration, just to live is holy.

It is the reality of interiority meeting interiority, an encounter of two spirits that is important. In any lesser meeting that bowl may just end up with peanuts in it.

That is art and the spirit of the tea bowl. Harmony, tranquility, prayer, respect will not come out of them if they do not go into them. It is an ongoing vision quest to make a spirit-filled tea bowl because it is an ongoing vision quest to make a spirit-filled person — a spirit-filled world.

A final adieu to this year, looking back with gratitude and forward with hope, I wish you many blessings in the next year.

JANUARY

1

2

3

4

5

6

Tea Bowl, Ice Crackle, Iron Yellow Glaze, 3 x 5¾ x 5¾", TH1587

it is one thing to be intelligent,

it is quite another thing to be wise.

J A N U A R Y

7

8

9

10

11

12

TEA BOWL, square form, Tenmoku with Crystal Rutile Glaze, $3\frac{1}{4}$ x $4\frac{5}{8}$ x $4\frac{5}{8}$", TH1547

There is a luminescence when something that transcends all of us, binds us together, differences and all.

J A N U A R Y

13

14

15

16

17

18

TEA BOWL, Iron Yellow Glaze, 3½ x 4¾ x 4¾", TH1567

o be a man of peace, you have to be a fighter.

J A N U A R Y

19

20

21

22

23

24

T he thing we all strive for is to shape our humanity in the image of God, to do good, stand up for what is true, create what is beautiful, and live for what unites and does not divide.

J A N U A R Y

25

26

27

28

29

30

31

Tea Bowl, "Kairagi" Glaze, $3\frac{1}{4}$ x $5\frac{3}{4}$ x $5\frac{3}{4}$", TH1574

Whoever said, "When you are doing what you love to do, you never work a day in your life" – that is correct.

FEBRUARY

1

2

3

4

5

6

TEA BOWL, Celadon, Gray Green with Iron Wash Glaze, 3¹/₈ x 5 x 5", TH1566

i

t is amazing how much art depends on "seeing". There are people who look but do not see, people who listen but do not hear, people who read but do not understand.

FEBRUARY

7

8

9

10

11

12

We certainly do live life forward, and understand it backwards.

F E B R V A R Y

13

14

15

16

17

18

Tea Bowl, Copper Red on Blue Celadon Glaze, 3½ x 4½ x 4½", TH1554

T here are never words without experiences, but there are many experiences without words.

FEBRUARY

19

20

21

22

23

24

TEA BOWL, "Clair de Lune" Glaze, 2⅞ x 5¼ x 5¼", TH1562

P eople of blessing encourage me to stretch and grow in my work at a time when it is tempting to retreat.

F E B R U A R Y

25

26

27

28

29

P erhaps in the end, knowing what
you do not like helps to shape what
you like.

MARCH

1

2

3

4

5

6

TEA BOWL, Molybdenum Glaze, $3\frac{1}{4}$ x $5\frac{1}{2}$ x $5\frac{1}{2}$", TH1556

it is gratitude and generosity that
make a great soul.

MARCH

7

8

9

10

11

12

Celebration Cup, Honan Tenmoku Glaze, 4 x 4¼ x 4¼", TH1584

The beauty of the spider's web comes out of the beauty of the spider's spirit.

MARCH

13

14

15

16

17

18

TEA BOWL, Copper Red Matte Glaze, 3½ x 4¾ x 4¾", TH1553

intuition gains strength when you trust in it often enough.

M A R C H

19

20

21

22

23

24

TEA BOWL, square form, Brown Armenian Bole Glaze, $3\frac{1}{2}$ x $5\frac{1}{8}$ x $5\frac{1}{8}$", TH1569

S ometimes I think the only real sin

is refusal to grow.

MARCH

25

26

27

28

29

30

31

TEA BOWL, Molybdenum Glaze, 3 x 5⅜ x 5⅜", TH1555

it is one thing to be able to write, it is quite another to have something "universal" to say.

APRIL

1

2

3

4

5

6

There is a unity of creative experience that cuts through the differences of the medium.

APRIL

7

8

9

10

11

12

TEA BOWL, square form, Honan Tenmoku Glaze, 3 x 4½ x 4½", TH1545

When we abandon tradition and culture, there are no honest roots for creativity.

A P R I L

13

14

15

16

17

18

it is amazing how our shadows fall in

places we ourselves cannot go.

A P R I L

19

20

21

22

23

24

TEA BOWL, Celadon, Blue Green Glaze, $3\frac{1}{8}$ x $5\frac{1}{2}$ x $5\frac{1}{2}$", TH1563

What there is still to see we have not yet dreamed of.

A P R I L

25

26

27

28

29

30

t is right to question everything but foolish to deny anything.

M A Y

1	
2	
3	
4	
5	
6	

TEA BOWL, Molybdenum Glaze, 3 x 5⅛ x 5⅜", TH1560

R isking and dreaming are primary

acts of creativity.

M A Y

7

8

9

10

11

12

The only antidote to hopelessness
is hope itself.

M A Y

13

14

15

16

17

18

TEA BOWL, Copper Red Glaze, 3 x 5⅜ x 5⅜", TH1549

K nowing the truth is not enough.

We have to "be" the truth.

M A Y

19

20

21

22

23

24

TEA BOWL, "Teadust" Glaze, 3½ x 4¾ x 4¾", TH1591

i t is unnatural to forget

how to play!

MAY

25

26

27

28

29

30

31

TEA BOWL, "Kairagi" Glaze, 3 x 6¼ x 6¼", TH1573

Another year to catch all of our
dreams – or at least make a dent
in them.

JUNE

1

2

3

4

5

6

TEA BOWL, Molybdenum Glaze, 3 x 5¾ x 5¾", TH1559

To give thanks is elemental prayer.

J U N E

7	

8	

9	

10	

11	

12	

The sign of a great soul is forgiveness, not revenge.

j u n e

13

14

15

16

17

18

Tea Bowl, Iron Yellow with Black Glaze, 3½ x 5¾ x 5¾", TH1391

he Lord's ways may indeed be

mysterious, but his timing is perfect.

J U N E

19

20

21

22

23

24

TEA BOWL, Opal Blues and Red Glaze, 2¾ x 6 x 6", TH1281

All of our worst agonies begin
with silence.

J U N E

25

26

27

28

29

30

S ome seeds never live to see the
flower, but the seeds of the spirit do.

J U L Y

1

2

3

4

5

6

We are all born with a soul,

but we have to acquire a spirit.

j u l y

7

8

9

10

11

12

TEA BOWL, Copper Blue Glaze, 3 x 6 x 6", TH1380

Living is not one thing and
prayer another.

j u l y

13

14

15

16

17

18

TEA BOWL, square form, "Hare's Fur" Glaze, 3 x 4¼ x 4¼", TH1572

rt is only a means when there is
something interior to share and
when there is not, it is not art, just
another thing.

J U L Y

19

20

21

22

23

24

TEA BOWL, White Glaze with Turquoise and Red, 3½ x 6 x 6", TH1280

he inner road is the only road that will humanize the world.

J U L Y

25

26

27

28

29

30

31

S ome doors only open from the inside and creating the human is one of them.

A u g u s t

1	

2	

3	

4	

5	

6	

TEA BOWL, square form, Tessah Glaze, $3\frac{3}{4}$ x $4\frac{3}{4}$ x $4\frac{3}{4}$", TH1568

here is only one thing that
measures art, and that is freedom.

Augu∫t

7

8

9

10

11

12

Tea Bowl, square form, Honan Tenmoku with Kaki Glaze, 2³⁄₄ x 4¹⁄₂ x 4¹⁄₂", TH1546

We should live and love wisely,

not perfectly!

August

13

14

15

16

17

18

TEA BOWL, Copper Red with Blue Celadon Glaze, 3¾ x 5 x 5", TH1398

o remember is to believe.

A u g u s t

19

20

21

22

23

24

R|eal knowledge is a virtue
of the heart.

A u g u s t

25

26

27

28

29

30

31

Tea Bowl, Blue Black Elm Ash Glaze, $3\frac{1}{4}$ x $5\frac{5}{8}$ x $5\frac{5}{8}$", TH1586

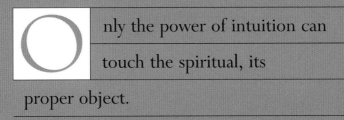

Only the power of intuition can touch the spiritual, its proper object.

S E P T E M B E R

1

2

3

4

5

6

TEA BOWL, Celadon, Gray-Green with Iron Orange Glaze, 3 x 5⅛ x 5⅛", TH1561

The only unlimited world is the world of the spiritual.

S E P T E M B E R

7

8

9

10

11

12

TEA BOWL, square form, Honan Tenmoku Glaze, $3\frac{1}{4}$ x $4\frac{3}{4}$ x $4\frac{3}{4}$", TH1544

F|reedom empowers us to be fully

human and to be humanly fulfilled.

SEPTEMBER

13

14

15

16

17

18

e have a tendency, an appetite for beauty which is from our very nature.

SEPTEMBER

19

20

21

22

23

24

Tea Bowl, Iron Blue Malt Glaze, 3¼ x 4¾ x 4¾", TH1571

E

vents are the currents
of possibility.

S E P T E M B E R

25

26

27

28

29

30

TEA BOWL, Celadon with Iron Yellow Glaze, 3½ x 5 x 5", TH1277

The routine of life holds us in
readiness for the events of the soul.

OCTOBER

1	
2	
3	
4	
5	
6	

TEA BOWL, Iron Blue Glaze, 3$\frac{1}{4}$ x 5$\frac{1}{4}$ x 5$\frac{1}{4}$", TH1577

i think that we will never lose the presence of the other within us, once formed it becomes part of our own fabric.

OCTOBER

7

8

9

10

11

12

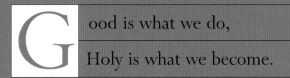

G ood is what we do,

Holy is what we become.

OCTOBER

13

14

15

16

17

18

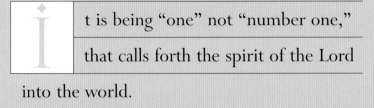

i t is being "one" not "number one," that calls forth the spirit of the Lord into the world.

OCTOBER

19

20

21

22

23

24

here is no excuse to be less than
we can be.

O C T O B E R

25

26

27

28

29

30

31

TEA BOWL, "Kairagi" Glaze, 3½ x 5¼ x 5¼", TH1575

Anyone who has not felt God's concern for unity, oneness of all his creation, does not know the living God.

ΠOVEMBER

1

2

3

4

5

6

TEA BOWL, Celadon, Green with Iron Yellow Glaze, $3\frac{1}{4}$ x $4\frac{3}{4}$ x $4\frac{3}{4}$", TH1565

Artists fight against tradition when they have nothing to add to it.

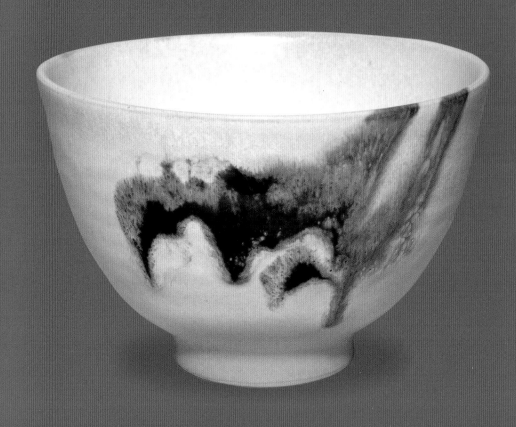

ΠOVEMBER

7

8

9

10

11

12

TEA BOWL, Molybdenum Glaze, 3½ x 5½ x 5½", TH1557

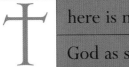here is nothing in the world so like
God as silence.

NOVEMBER

13

14

15

16

17

18

TEA BOWL, Copper Red Glaze, 3 x 5¾ x 5¾", TH1551

here is no sin in being down, it is staying down that kills.

ΠOVEMBER

19

20

21

22

23

24

TEA BOWL, Celadon, Lavender Glaze, 3¾ x 6 x 6", TH1564

A "mitzvah" is like the birth of a new angel – a messenger of God. It is not so mystical, not so mythical, not so magical – just good and the good has wings.

NOVEMBER

25

26

27

28

29

30

TEA BOWL, Armenian Bole Glaze, 3½ x 4¾ x 4¾", TH1376

he need for interior rest is just as important as physical rest.

December

1

2

3

4

5

6

L ive each day in the daily details of

loving kindness and caring.

DECEMBER

7

8

9

10

11

12

TEA BOWL, square form, Honan Tenmoku Glaze, $3\frac{1}{4}$ x $4\frac{3}{8}$ x $4\frac{3}{8}$", TH1543 ·

**W**here the mountain meets the
sea is always worth the trip.

Decemberᴿ

13

14

15

16

17

18

Tᴇᴀ Bᴏᴡʟ, Copper Red Glaze, 3 x 5¼ x 5¼", TH1550

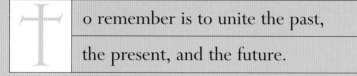

To remember is to unite the past, the present, and the future.

DECEMBER

19

20

21

22

23

24

TEA BOWL, square form, Iron Yellow Glaze, 3½ x 4⅝ x 4⅝ ", TH1580

L ove is the best healer; in the end,
it may be the only healer.

DECEMBER

25

26

27

28

29

30

31

TEA BOWL, square form, Elm Ash Glaze, $3\frac{5}{8}$ x $4\frac{1}{2}$ x $4\frac{1}{2}$", TH1579

THIS IS THE DAY THAT THE LORD HAS MADE.
LET US REJOICE AND BE GLAD THEREIN.
Psalm 118:24

This passage from Psalms is read at the celebration of the New Moon; the beginning of each month. The emphasis on the importance of each day, each month, each year, is most appropriate as an introduction to this publication: *Celebrate the Days: Ceramic works by Brother Thomas.*

Brother Thomas' teabowls are all works filled with a life affirming spirit and commitment to appreciating the gift of Life.

To view one of his creations, to read his words of wisdom, to record important moments in Life – all are part of this publication. It is with a sense of gratitude that we share *Celebrate the Days* with you.

– BHP, SFP
2000

B rother Thomas Bezanson, an American citizen, was born in Halifax, Nova Scotia in 1929. He was a Benedictine monk at Weston Priory, Weston, VT, for twenty-five years and has worked as an artist-in-residence with the Benedictine sisters of Erie since 1985. Thomas' porcelains can be found in over fifty national and international public collections, including the Metropolitan Museum of Art, New York, the Art Institute of Chicago, the Victoria and Albert Museum, London, the Renwick Gallery of the Smithsonian Institute, Washington, D.C., the Osaka Municipal Museum, and the Museum of Fine Arts, Boston. The work is also in numerous private collections in the U.S. and abroad. Brother Thomas is represented by the Pucker Gallery, Boston.